About Passover

The Passover Table

Festival Candles
Wine/Grape Juice
Kiddush Cups
Haggadot

Miriam's cup
Elijah's Cup
Salt Water

Three Matzot

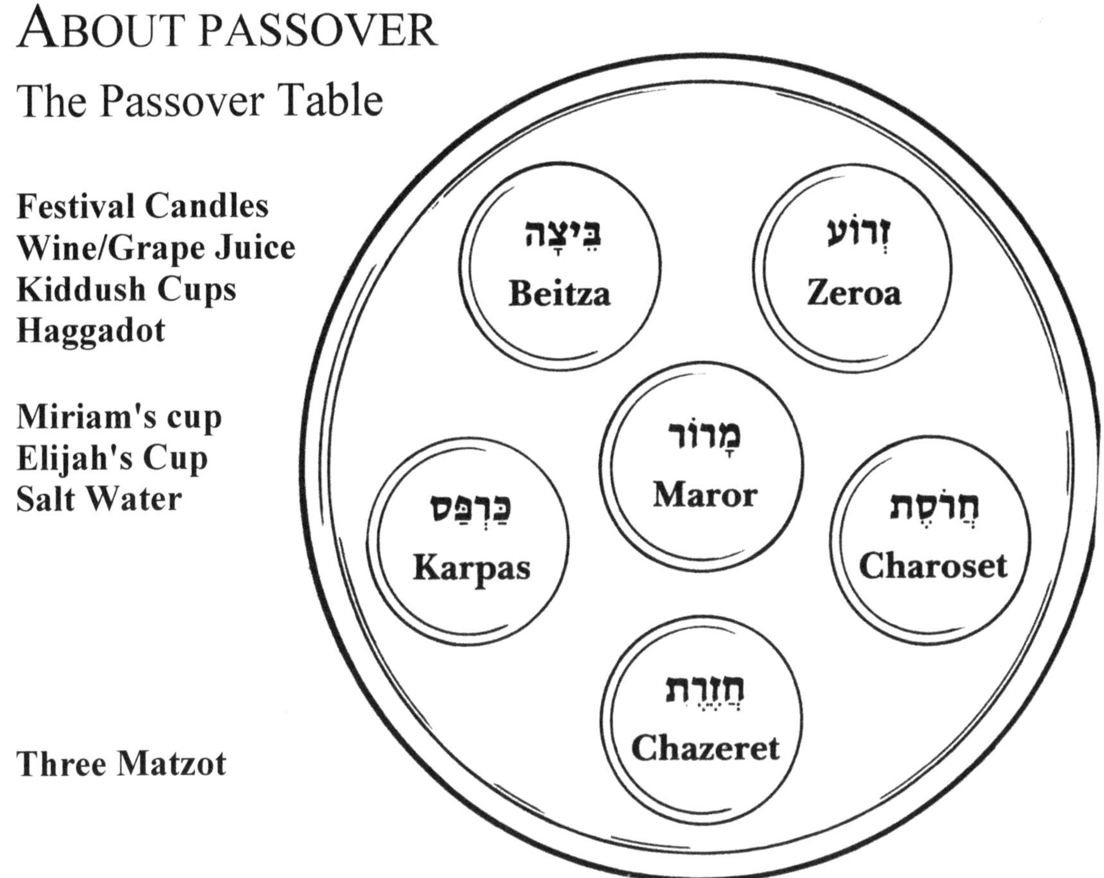

Seder Plate:

Charoset: Mixture of apples, nuts, wine and spices.
Zeroa: Shankbone, roasted or a beet, roasted
Beitza: Roasted hardboiled egg.
Karpas: Vegetable such as parsley or a potato
Maror: Bitter herbs horseradish root or prepared horseradish
Chazeret: Bitter vegetable such as celery or romaine lettuce

Introduction

Passover is the most widely observed Jewish holiday. On Passover, Jews all over the world conduct Passover Seders. A Passover Seder is a festive meal that combines discussion and story telling with symbolism and ritual. The many unusual foods and customs included were originally designed to make the participants, especially the children, curious about the meaning of Passover. Typically all present at a Passover Seder participate. Thus Passover is also a celebration of the power of the family to keep the Jewish tradition alive. It accomplishes this in part by emphasizing how the history of the Jews is connected to the religious beliefs and practices that define the Jews as a distinct people.

Seder means order, organization. It is an example of how discipline prevents freedom from disintegrating into chaos. As free people we recognize the need to provide structures within which we have the freedom to improvise. During Passover Seders we are encouraged to digress and to discuss, to teach and to learn from one another. The order of the Seder ensures that all the significant details that are associated with Passover are included. The Seder was never supposed to be recited by rote. Long before printed books and formal schools, the purpose of the yearly Seder was to transform every Jewish home into a classroom as well as a forum for discussion. The guidelines for this structured interactive learning and the text that stimulates discussion was provided by the Haggadah

Haggadah (from the Hebrew root "to tell") means to narrate. The Haggadah is the special book used for the Seder service. It contains the story of the Exodus from Egypt, explanations of symbolic objects on the Seder table, and prayers, psalms, and Passover songs. The Haggadah guides the Seder participants through a fixed progression of 15 carefully orchestrated steps. Although the length and the contents of these steps can vary, the order of these steps is significant and each step is essential. The Sages say that Passover occurs on the 15th of Nissan, to teach us that just as the moon waxes for 15 days, so too our growth must be in 15 gradual steps.

The 15 steps of the Passover Seder:

Prologue	Hadlakat ha-Nerot (Lighting the Festival Candles)
1. Kadesh:	Kiddush is said, drink the first cup of wine.
2. Ur'Chatz:	Wash hands
3. Karpas:	Dip vegetables in salt water, say blessing
4. Yachatz	Break the middle matzah and hide the afikomen
5. Maggid	Recite the four questions, tell the story of Passover, drink the second cup of wine, honor Miriam
6. Rochtzah	Wash hands, say blessing
7. Motzi	Blessing for bread
8. Matzah	Blessing for matzah
9. Marror	Dip bitter herb in charoset, say blessing
10. Korech	Eat sandwich of matzah and bitter herbs
11. Shulchan Aruch	Eat festive meal
12. Tzafun	Eat afikomen
13. Barech	Blessing after eating, drink third cup of wine, welcome Elijah the prophet
14. Hallel	Sing songs of praise, drink the fourth cup of wine
15. Nirtzah.	Conclude the Seder
Epilogue	Sing songs

Historical Overview

The original Haggadah was a product of a Jewish generation wrenched from its roots and splintered within its ranks. Previously the nature of Judaism had been clear. It was a religion whose festivities revolved around a serious of acts performed by a priestly class within the precincts of the Jerusalem Temple. Pilgrims to Jerusalem spent Passover eve recounting the tale of the Exodus and consuming the lamb, which they had sacrificed in the Temple that afternoon. The celebration was unstructured with no elaborate order of prayer.

Two events conspired to alter this pattern. The first was the destruction of the second Temple by the Romans in the year 70 CE. The second was the splintering of the Jewish community into disparate sects, one of which was early Christianity. The idea of using a Haggadah was introduced at this time and it transformed the Passover celebration into a yearly gathering during which Jews recalled their past, reflected on their present circumstances and envisioned their future.

The Mishnah, compiled at the turn of the third century of the common era, describes a Seder much like the traditional ones held today. Kiddush inaugurated the celebration. Children were urged to ask questions about the uniqueness of the meal. Their queries were answered with descriptions of the Exodus and commentary. The symbolism of the Seder was explained. Psalms of praise (Hallel) were chanted and a few finale prayers brought the Seder to a close.

Originally the Four Questions were not a fixed text for a child to recite. They were provided as sample questions which were directed at the child if the child's own natural inquisitiveness failed him (at the time only boys were addressed). So if the child asked nothing, he could be prompted by asking him, "Didn't you notice that we only have matzah tonight? Didn't you notice we are all reclining at the table?"

Even at this early date the Haggadah transcended a mere recounting of the past. As Jews marked their ancestor's deliverance from Egypt, they could not help but note the parallels to their current situations. So the Haggadah became the story of more than one period of persecution and salvation. The Pharaoh of the biblical period personified later oppressors, and the archetypal salvation from the Egyptians came to represent Israel's deliverance throughout the ages.

Later generations inherited the Haggadah of the Mishnah. Though they did not alter its essential nature, they did expand its contents. Throughout history Jews everywhere continued to include commentary which alluded to their present circumstances so that the story of the Exodus would be infused with contemporary relevance. The Haggadah we are using today is a product of this tradition. Even the use of English has a precedent since some of the most illustrious rabbis in history, including Rashi, translated all or part of their Haggadot into the vernacular. These rabbis understood that the Haggadah should be recited in a language that all present comprehend or the recitation will not have fulfilled its purpose.

THE PASSOVER SEDER

Welcome

Leader: Welcome to our Passover Seder. Now in the presence of loved ones and friends, we are gathered for our sacred celebration. Passover is the time when participation in a Passover Seder provides an opportunity to embark on a personal journey from slavery to freedom. The Haggadah will be our guidebook. The first part of the Seder deals with history. After the meal, the Seder continues so that we can express our faith and our hopes for the future.

In every generation, we must see ourselves as if we personally were liberated from Egypt. We gather tonight to tell the ancient story of a people's liberation from Egyptian slavery. This is the story of our origins as a people. It is from these events that we gain our ethics, our vision of history, our dreams for the future. We gather tonight, as have two hundred generations of Jewish families before us, to retell the timeless tale.

Our tradition requires that on Seder night, we do more than just tell the story. We must live the story. Tonight, we will re-experience the liberation from Egypt. We will remember how our family suffered as slaves; we will feel the exhilaration of redemption. We must re-taste the bitterness and must rejoice over our newfound freedom. We remember slavery in order to deepen our commitment to end all suffering; we recreate our liberation in order to reinforce our commitment to universal freedom.

For our children, and for the children within us, we need to make our stories vivid. And so, tonight, our table is a stage. The Seder is like a play. This Hagaddah will be our script. The Seder plate, the matzah and the wine are the props that we will use to bring life to the story

We begin our Seder with the lighting of Holiday Candles.

Lighting the Festival Candles

Leader: By lighting the candles we make this home into a sanctuary, a place that cannot be penetrated by the things that preoccupy us and distract us as we attend to all of our details of daily lives.

(the candles are lit)

Women and/or Group (on Shabbat add the words in brackets):

בָּרוּךְ אַתָּה יְיָ אֱלֹהֵינוּ מֶלֶךְ הָעוֹלָם
אֲשֶׁר קִדְּשָׁנוּ בְּמִצְוֹתָיו וְצִוָּנוּ
לְהַדְלִיק נֵר שֶׁל (שַׁבָּת וְשֶׁל) יוֹם טוֹב.

Baruch Atah Adonai
Eloheinu Melech ha-olam,
asher kid-shanu b'mitz-vo-tav,
v'tzi-vanu l'hadlik ner
shel (shabbat v'shel) yom tov.

Leader: Something greater then ourselves can be symbolized by the light of a candle. Every holy light we kindle helps to banish hatred and bigotry by bringing light the world.

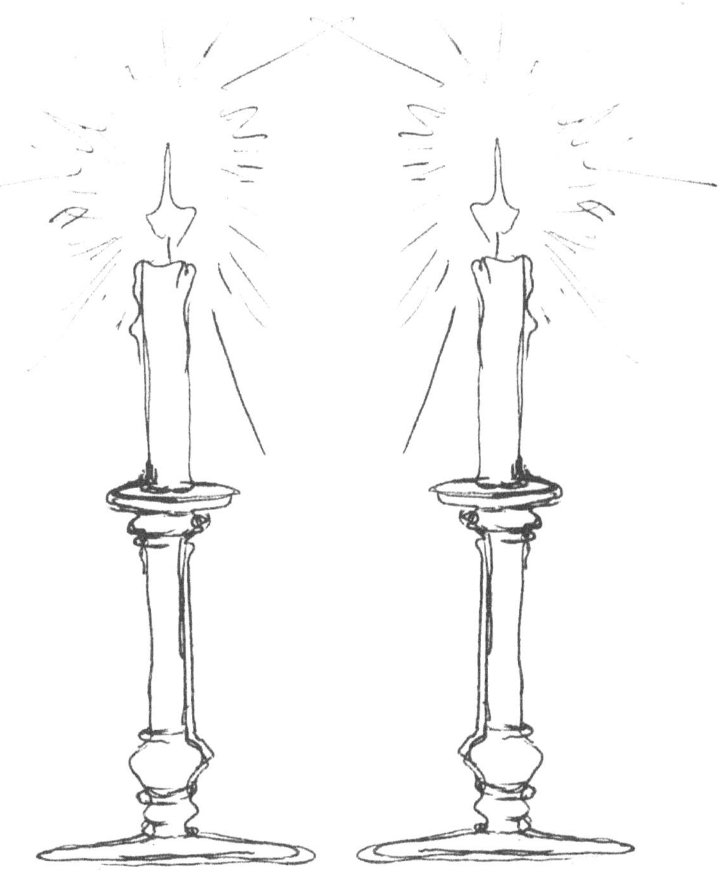

The Four Cups of Wine

Leader: Tonight we will drink four cups of wine.

Participant: It has been said that the four cups represent the four corners of the universe, because we seek freedom everywhere;

Participant: It has been said that the four cups represent the four types of freedom, physical freedom, intellectual freedom, emotional freedom and spiritual freedom;

Participant: It has been said that the four cups symbolize the four seasons of the year, because freedom must be scrupulously guarded at all times;

Participant: It has been said the four cups represent the four ancient empires that tyrannized Israel and have since passed away, because there will come a time when tyranny will pass away once and for all;

Participant: It has been said the four cups each recall the four statements made by God describing the four stages of liberation. In Exodus we read that the Jews would be brought out of Egypt, delivered from slavery, redeemed with an outstretched arm and made into a great nation.

KADDESH, Sanctifying Freedom

The First Cup

Leader: Not all people enjoy the freedoms we cherish. Many in our world still seek physical freedom from oppression and degradation. We dedicate the first cup of wine to them. May we soon share our freedom and our joy with them, and may the sweet taste of the wine remind us of our responsibilities toward them.

(all stand and raise cups)

Leader: We take up the first cup and proclaim
the holiness of this Day of Freedom!

Group (on Shabbat say words in brackets):

(וַיְהִי־עֶרֶב וַיְהִי־בֹקֶר יוֹם הַשִּׁשִּׁי.
וַיְכֻלּוּ הַשָּׁמַיִם וְהָאָרֶץ וְכָל־צְבָאָם. וַיְכַל אֱלֹהִים בַּיּוֹם הַשְּׁבִיעִי מְלַאכְתּוֹ אֲשֶׁר עָשָׂה, וַיִּשְׁבֹּת בַּיּוֹם הַשְּׁבִיעִי מִכָּל־מְלַאכְתּוֹ אֲשֶׁר עָשָׂה. וַיְבָרֶךְ אֱלֹהִים אֶת־יוֹם הַשְּׁבִיעִי וַיְקַדֵּשׁ אֹתוֹ, כִּי בוֹ שָׁבַת מִכָּל־מְלַאכְתּוֹ אֲשֶׁר בָּרָא אֱלֹהִים לַעֲשׂוֹת.)

(vay'hi erev vay'hi voker yom hashishi. Vay'chulu hashamayim v'ha'aretz v'chol tz'va'am. Vay'chal Elohim bayom hash'vi'I m'lachto asher asah. Vayishbot bayom hash'vi'I mikol m'lachto asher asah. Vay'varech Elohim et yom hash'vi'I vay'kadesh oto, ki vo shavat mikol m'lachto asher bara Elohim la'asot)

בָּרוּךְ אַתָּה יְיָ אֱלֹהֵינוּ מֶלֶךְ הָעוֹלָם בּוֹרֵא פְּרִי הַגָּפֶן.

Baruch Atah Adonai Eloheinu Melech ha-olam, borei p'ri ha-gafen.

We praise You, The Source of All That Exists,
Who creates the fruit of the vine!

(all drink the first cup or continue with long kiddush on the following page)

Participant or Group (optional):

בָּרוּךְ אַתָּה יְיָ אֱלֹהֵינוּ מֶלֶךְ הָעוֹלָם אֲשֶׁר בָּחַר בָּנוּ מִכָּל־עָם וְרוֹמְמָנוּ מִכָּל־לָשׁוֹן וְקִדְּשָׁנוּ בְּמִצְוֹתָיו. וַתִּתֶּן־לָנוּ יְיָ אֱלֹהֵינוּ בְּאַהֲבָה (שַׁבָּתוֹת לִמְנוּחָה וּ)מוֹעֲדִים לְשִׂמְחָה חַגִּים וּזְמַנִּים לְשָׂשׂוֹן אֶת־יוֹם (הַשַּׁבָּת הַזֶּה וְאֶת־יוֹם) חַג הַמַּצּוֹת הַזֶּה, זְמַן חֵרוּתֵנוּ, (בְּאַהֲבָה) מִקְרָא קֹדֶשׁ זֵכֶר לִיצִיאַת מִצְרָיִם. כִּי בָנוּ בָחַרְתָּ וְאוֹתָנוּ קִדַּשְׁתָּ מִכָּל־הָעַמִּים (וְשַׁבָּת) וּמוֹעֲדֵי קָדְשְׁךָ (בְּאַהֲבָה וּבְרָצוֹן) בְּשִׂמְחָה וּבְשָׂשׂוֹן הִנְחַלְתָּנוּ. בָּרוּךְ אַתָּה יְיָ מְקַדֵּשׁ (הַשַּׁבָּת וְ)יִשְׂרָאֵל וְהַזְּמַנִּים.

Baruch atah Adonai, Eloheinu melech ha-olam, asher bachar banu mikol am, v'rom'manu mikol lashon, v'kid'shanu b'mitzvotav. Va'titen lanu Adonai Eloheinu b'ahava, mo'adim l'simcha, chagim u-z'manim l'sason. Et yom chag ha-matzot ha-zeh, z'man cheiruteinu, mikra kodesh, zecher litziyat Mitzrayim. Ki vanu vacharta, v'otanu kidashta mikol ha-amim. U'mo'adei kodsheh'cha b'simcha u-v'sason hin'chaltanu. Baruch atah Adonai m'kadesh Yisrael v'ha-z'manim.

We praise You, The Source of All That Exists, who creates the fruit of the vine! You have called us for service from among the peoples, and have hallowed our lives with commandments. In love You have given us festivals for rejoicing, seasons of celebration, this Festival of Matzot, the time of our freedom, a day of sacred assembly commemorating the Exodus from *Mitzrayim*. Praised are You, who gave us this joyful heritage and who sanctifies the people of Israel, and the festival days.

(All drink the first cup)

The She-heh-che-yanu.

Leader: Now we say the blessing that reminds us of the continuous wonder of being alive, the she-heh-che-yanu.

Group:

בָּרוּךְ אַתָּה יְיָ אֱלֹהֵינוּ מֶלֶךְ הָעוֹלָם
שֶׁהֶחֱיָנוּ וְקִיְּמָנוּ וְהִגִּיעָנוּ לַזְּמַן הַזֶּה.

Baruch Atah Adonai
Eloheinu Melech ha-olam,
she-heh-che-yanu, v'ki-y'manu,
v'higi-anu lazman hazeh.

We praise You,
The Source of All That Exists,
who has given us life and sustenance,
kept us alive, and brought us
to this moment
(so we may celebrate this season of joy).

UR'CHATZ, Washing the Hands

Leader: Slaves eat quickly, stopping neither to wash nor to reflect. Tonight, we are free. So we can take our time. So we will pause now to wash our hands, but since we will not be eating just yet, we won't recite the hand-washing blessing.

(Some or all of the participants leave the table to wash. Or pass a bowl of warm water, a small cup and a towel around the table so that everyone can pour three cupfuls over their fingers)

KARPAS, Rebirth and Renewal

Leader: Even before the Exodus from Egypt each spring our people celebrated at this time of year. Like all people, our people in ancient times celebrated the liberation of the earth itself from wintry darkness, and rejoiced in the yearly rebirth of nature. Therefore in the spring of the year, the season of rebirth and renewal, on the festival Pesach, we read from the Song of Songs.

Song of Songs

Shir ha-shirim. Asher l'shloymo — The song of songs ascribed to Soloman

Yisha-keyni min-shikos p'hu — Kisses me with the kisses of his mouth

K'tovim dodey-cha mi-oyim. — Better is his love than wine

Leader's spouse or participant:
Come, my beloved, my lovely one, come.
Behold, winter is past, the rains are over and gone.
Flowers appear on the earth.
The season for singing has come,
and the song of the turtledove is heard in our land.
The fig tree is forming its first green figs
and the blossoming vines smell oh so grand.
Come then, my beloved, my lovely one, come.

Leader's spouse or participant:
Come, my beloved, let us go to the fields.
We'll spend the night in the village,
and in early morn we'll visit the vineyards.
We'll see if the grapes have blossomed,
if the pomegranate trees are in flower.
For then shall I give you the gift of my love.

Leader: The karpas also reminds us of springtime and hope. Sometimes we despair of the evil in our world. Pesach calls us to hope again. Now we dip the karpas in salt water. We are reminded that both the tender greens of the earth and the salts of the seas need to be joined together to sustain life. And, because tears taste salty, we also remember the tears our people cried in Egypt when they were slaves.

(Distribute greens)
(Each person dips some greens in salt water)

Group:

בָּרוּךְ אַתָּה יְיָ אֱלֹהֵינוּ
מֶלֶךְ הָעוֹלָם בּוֹרֵא פְּרִי הָאֲדָמָה.

Baruch Atah Adonai
Eloheinu Melech ha-olam,
borei p'ri ha-adamah.

We praise You,
The Source of All That Exists
Who creates the fruit of the earth.

(Eat the greens)

(Fill the second cup of wine)

YACHATZ, Breaking the Matzah

Leader: (uncover the matzot and break the middle matzah). We take the middle of the three matzot and break it in two. One part we keep here. The other part we shall hide. This is called the "afikomen" from a Greek word that means dessert. Anyone is welcome to hunt for it and whoever finds it will be rewarded. When the hidden part is found we will put the two halves together again to symbolize that what is broken off is not really lost to our people so long as we remember and search. Later we will share it, just as in days of old when the Paschal lamb offering itself was shared during this service at the Temple in Jerusalem. Among people everywhere, sharing of bread forms a bond of fellowship.

(The afikomen is hidden. Participants may search for it and whoever finds it can withhold it. During the second part of the Seder the afikomen can be exchanged for a gift to recall the gifts bestowed on the departing Hebrews by the Egyptian civilians.)

Leader: (Hold aloft the plate with the uncovered matzot) We will now recite the call to Passover:

Group: This is the bread of affliction, which our ancestors ate in Egypt.
Let all who are hungry come and eat.
Let all who are in need come and celebrate the Passover.
This year we are here; next year may we be in Israel.
This year we are still enslaved; next year may we be free.

Leader (optional): Let us repeat, the call to Passover in ancient Aramaic,.

Group (optional): *Ha lachma anya dee a-cha-lu a-va-ha-sa-na b'ara d'mitzrayim.*

הָא לַחְמָא עַנְיָא דִּי אֲכַלוּ אַבְהָתַנָא בְּאַרְעָא דְמִצְרָיִם.

Leader (optional): This is the bread of affliction that our ancestors ate as slaves in the land of Egypt.

Group (optional): *Kol dichfin yay-say v'yaychul; kol ditzrich yay-say v'yifsach.*

כָּל־דִכְפִין יֵיתֵי וְיֵכֹל, כָּל־דִצְרִיךְ יֵיתֵי וְיִפְסַח.

Leader (optional): Let all who are hungry come and eat. Let all who are in need share come and join this Passover celebration.

Group (optional): *Ha-shata hacha, l'shana ha-ba'ah b'ara d'Yisrael.*

הָשַׁתָּא הָכָא, לַשָּׁנָה הַבָּאָה בְּאַרְעָא דְיִשְׂרָאֵל.

Leader (optional): This year we are here. Next year may we be in the land of Israel.

Group (optional): *Ha-shata avday, l'shanah ha-ba'ah b'nay chorin.*

הָשַׁתָּא עַבְדֵי, לַשָּׁנָה הַבָּאָה בְּנֵי חוֹרִין.

Leader (optional): This year we are all still enslaved. Next year may all be free.

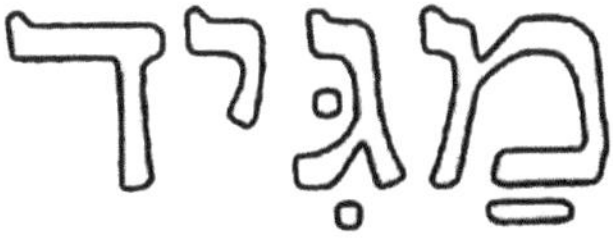

MAGGID, Telling the Story

Leader: Why do we tell stories? To answer questions. Why do we ask questions? Because we are curious about who we are and the world we see around us. Questioning is a sign of freedom, proof that we are free to investigate, to analyze, to satisfy our intellectual curiosity. The Talmud states that anyone can ask questions; the youngest, the oldest, even a scholar at the table of scholars.

The Four Questions

A child or any inquisitive person:
Why is this night different from all other nights?

1. On all other nights we eat both leavened bread and unleavened bread; why on this night do we eat only unleavened bread?
2. On all other nights we eat all kinds of herbs and vegetables; why on this night do we eat especially bitter herbs and vegetables?
3. On all other nights we do not usually dip our foods even once; why on this night do we dip twice?
4. On all other nights we sit up straight when we eat; why on this night do we recline on pillows?

מַה נִּשְׁתַּנָּה הַלַּיְלָה הַזֶּה מִכָּל הַלֵּילוֹת.

שֶׁבְּכָל הַלֵּילוֹת אָנוּ אוֹכְלִין חָמֵץ וּמַצָּה, הַלַּיְלָה הַזֶּה כֻּלּוֹ מַצָּה.

שֶׁבְּכָל הַלֵּילוֹת אָנוּ אוֹכְלִין שְׁאָר יְרָקוֹת, הַלַּיְלָה הַזֶּה מָרוֹר.

שֶׁבְּכָל הַלֵּילוֹת אֵין אָנוּ מַטְבִּילִין אֲפִילוּ פַּעַם אֶחָת, הַלַּיְלָה הַזֶּה שְׁתֵּי פְעָמִים.

שֶׁבְּכָל הַלֵּילוֹת אָנוּ אוֹכְלִין בֵּין יוֹשְׁבִין וּבֵין מְסֻבִּין, הַלַּיְלָה הַזֶּה כֻּלָּנוּ מְסֻבִּין.

Mah nishtanah ha-lahylah ha-zeh mi-kol ha-layloht, mi-kol ha-layloht?

She-b'khol ha-layloht anu okhlin sh'ar y'rakot, sh'ar y'rakot.
Ha-lahylah ha-zeh, ha-lahylah ha-zeh, maror.

She-b'khol ha-layloht anu okhlin chameytz u-matzah, chameytz u-matzah.
Ha-lahylah ha-zeh, ha-lahylah ha-zeh, kooloh matzah.

She-b'khol ha-layloht ayn anu mat'bilin afilu pa'am echat, afilu pa'am echat.
Ha-lahylah ha-zeh, ha-lahylah ha-zeh, sh'tay p'amim.

She-b'khol ha-layloht anu okhlin bayn yosh'bin u'vayn m'soobin, bayn yosh'bin u'vayn m'soobin.
Ha-lahylah ha-zeh, ha-lahylah ha-zeh, koolanu m'soobin.

Group:

עֲבָדִים הָיִינוּ

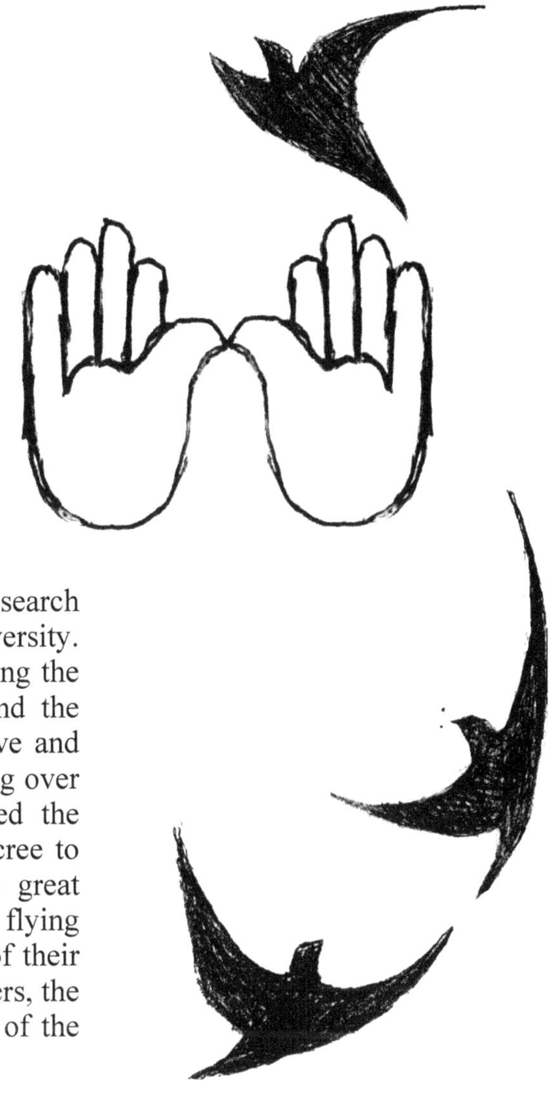

Avadiym hayinu. We were slaves of Pharaoh in Egypt, and the Lord our God brought us out from there with a mighty hand and an outstretched arm. If God had not brought our ancestors out from Egypt, then even we, our children, and our children's children might still be enslaved to Pharaoh in Egypt. Therefore, even if we were all wise, all old, all steady, all learned in the ways of God, it would still be incumbent upon us to tell the story of the departure from Egypt.

Participant (optional): It is important to search for meaning even in the midst of great adversity. Therefore we remember that long ago, during the first century, five great scholars sat around the Seder table at B'nai Berak one Passover eve and read the words of the Haggadah, deliberating over their meaning. The Romans had destroyed the Temple. It was in violation of Roman decree to study or teach, but there they sat--these great scholars--unmindful of the hours that were flying by. The meeting broke up only when one of their students came and said to them, "Our teachers, the time has already come to recite the Sh'ma of the morning service."

Participant (optional): The struggle for freedom, for the elusive rights of life, liberty and the pursuit of justice, is a constant one. In every age, some new freedom is won and established, adding to the advancement of human happiness and security. Yet each age creates more Pharaohs and more enslavements, requiring new liberations. The victory over the first Pharaoh in Egypt was but the beginning, a foreshadowing of all the emancipations that were to follow, and which will yet follow in the days to come. Mitzrayim means the narrow place, the place that squeezes the life out of a human soul and body. We are all still enslaved in Mitzrayim, because we are all still struggling to be free. We retell and expand upon the story of our Exodus from Mitzrayim to remind us to continue to work for the time when all the Pharaohs of the world will be vanquished and all peoples will enjoy peace and freedom.

The Four Children

Leader: Four times the Torah bids us to retell the story of the Exodus from Egypt. Four times the Torah repeats: "And you shall tell your child on that day..." From this our tradition infers that there are four kinds of children. To each we respond in a different manner.

Participant: The wise child loves the holiday and wants to know all about it. This child might ask, "What are the observances which our God commanded us?" In response to this child we look for ways to increase her involvement in the Seder and explain the observances of the Passover and the symbolism thoroughly.

Participant: The scornful child does not understand what Passover has to do with her and asks, "What does this Seder mean to you?" By using the expression "to you" as if it does not concern her. To her we say: "Join us tonight. Be fully present, participate and listen closely. Then you will experience what the Seder means to us."

Participant: When the simple child questions, "What is this?" then we say, "We are remembering a time long ago in another land when we were forced to work for other people as slaves. With a mighty arm God made us a free people and we are celebrating our freedom." Growing older, learning more about our people, and observing the Seder year by year, this child too will come to love Passover and to appreciate its beauty and its message.

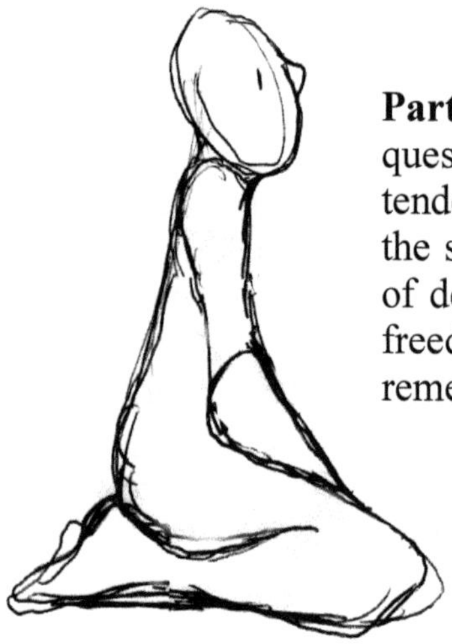

Participant: And with the child who doesn't think to question, we must take the initiative. With patience and tenderness we say, "This wondrous evening happens in the spring of every year, so we may remember how out of death and sorrow and slavery come life and joy and freedom. To remember the sorrow we eat bitter herbs; to remember the joy we drink sweet wine."

Leader: Let us now tell the story of the Exodus from Egypt. It is significant to note that the Haggadah originally described the oppression of the Egyptians, the misery of slavery, the ten plagues and the miraculous flight from Egypt without mentioning a single word about Moses. This was because Passover is a celebration of the Jewish people not a time to glorify a single individual. Moses was a great leader but he was only a messenger for something greater than himself. His role in the story is an example of how Divine Forces use human beings as conduits but it is essential to remember that it was a Force beyond human understanding that freed the Israelites, not Moses. Because the Talmudic rabbis were afraid that the people would make Moses into a supernatural being, which would confuse the meaning of Exodus, they left him out of the Haggadah. This Haggadah does include Moses because in modern times we have come to realize that the human side of the story needs to be told as well. By including both the human aspects and the miraculous occurrences, the story creates a more memorable impression. Furthermore we are reassured that freedom is possible; deliverance can come; salvation is within our reach; and the dream of redemption can become a reality. Within this story, and the human personalities that give the story its depth, we will search for deeper meanings and relevance to our own lives. Anyone is welcome to add commentary and midrash to this story as we go along.

The Passover Story

Participant: The Hebrew people first entered Egypt at the invitation of Pharaoh. Joseph, a Hebrew, had served for many years as overseer of all Pharaoh's lands and possessions. His wisdom and skill as an administrator increased Pharaoh's wealth and power considerably. When Joseph's family arrived Pharaoh invited them to live in Egypt as an acknowledgment of his gratitude to Joseph (and perhaps as a way to keep Joseph from leaving Egypt.)

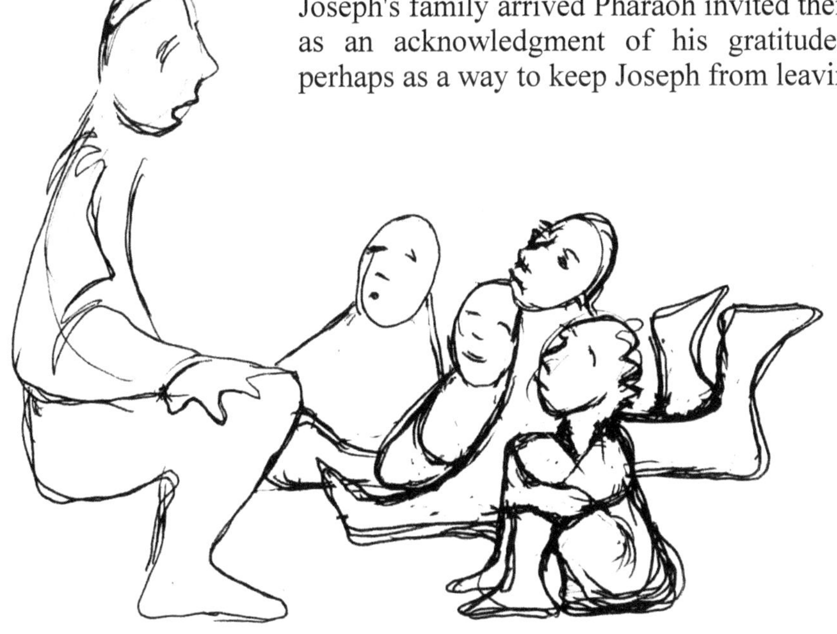

Participant: Years passed. The Hebrews became prosperous. Their numbers increased and they spread throughout the Egyptian Empire. They lived in peace and adopted Egyptian customs but still maintained their identity as Hebrews.

After many generations the Pharaohs of Egypt no longer remembered Joseph and how he saved the Egyptian people from famine and increased their wealth. One Pharaoh in particular worried that this large, prosperous group might join with Egypt's enemies in time of war. The Hebrews had committed no crime, nor had they been accused of any. Their mere existence as a numerous and prosperous people was viewed as a threat. So this Pharaoh began a campaign to systematically strip the Hebrews of their power and reduce their numbers.

Participant: Pharaoh forced the Hebrews to build huge granaries and store houses Taskmasters were appointed to beat and torture them. Over time they were enslaved and required to fulfill ever more impossible quotas and were beaten when unable to achieve them. "But the more they afflicted them, the more they multiplied and the more they spread abroad." This enraged Pharaoh. Finally he ordered that every newborn male Hebrew child be killed.

Participant: One mother, Jocheved, hid her baby boy for three months. When she could no longer keep the baby's existence secret, she placed him in a basket and put it in the reeds by the river near the bathing area of Pharaoh's daughter. Miriam, the baby's six-year-old sister, hid in the reeds near the royal bathing area and watched over her baby brother.

Participant: Soon Pharaoh's daughter came down to the river. She saw the ark and sent her handmaiden to fetch it. When she saw the crying baby inside she was moved with compassion. "This is one of the Hebrew's children" she said, and decided to save the baby. She called him Moses.

Participant: Miriam then ventured forward and approached the princess. She offered Jocheved, as nursemaid for the baby. The Princess hired Jocheved to raise the baby. Thus the child's own mother became his first teacher and he learned from her that he was a Hebrew and that the Hebrews believe in One God, a single Source of All that Exists. Moses stayed with his mother for several years until he was old enough to be brought him to Pharaoh's daughter who adopted him as her son.

Participant: From that point on Moses lived in the palace and was educated as an Egyptian prince. As he grew up he watched the suffering of the Hebrew slaves. One day as an adult, he became so angry as he watched a slave being beaten by a guard, so incensed by the injustice he was witnessing, that he struck the guard and killed him. This moment of anger ended Moses' life of privilege. He had committed an act that would be punished by his own execution if news of the deed reached Pharaoh. So Moses fled to Midian.

Participant: In Midian. Moses became a shepherd, married, and had children. One day while tending his sheep in the desert, Moses noticed a burning bush. As he approached the bush, he heard a voice calling, "Moses."
"Here I am," He answered.
"I am the God of your ancestors, Abraham, Isaac and Jacob, Sarah, Rebekah, Rachel and Leah. I have seen how the Egyptians oppress your people, the Hebrews. Therefore I am sending you to Pharaoh and you shall free the Hebrews from the Egyptians"

All sing (optional):
When Israel was in Egypt land,
"Let my people go!" "
Oppressed so hard they could not stand
"Let my people go!"

The Lord told Moses what to do,
Let my people go!"
To lead the children of Israel through,
"Let my people go!"

Go down, Moses, Way down in Egypt Land
Tell ol' Pharaoh: "Let my people go!"

Participant: Moses was unsure of himself. He said, "Who am I that I should go to Pharaoh? He will not listen to me, nor will the Children of Israel, the Hebrews. They will not believe that I, an ordinary man, am a messenger of God."
The voice answered, "I will be with you. And I will send your brother, Aaron to stand by your side and speak for you."

Participant: So Moses left Midian and returned to Egypt. On his way he met Aaron, his brother coming to meet him. Moses and Aaron went to see Pharaoh together. They said to Pharaoh, "the Lord God of Israel, the God of the Hebrews, has sent us to you, O Pharaoh, to tell you to let the people of Israel go."

Pharaoh was unmoved. He turned to Moses in anger. "Be gone!" he said, "Let us hear no more of this God of yours. You turn your people's thoughts from their work. Heavier work will be given to them. Then they will have no time to listen to your words."

Participant: Moses and Aaron warned Pharaoh, "The Lord God will send plague after plague to afflict you until you let the Hebrews, the Children of Israel, go".
And the next morning all the waters in the land of Egypt turned as red as blood.
For seven days the Egyptians had no water to drink. But Pharaoh was unimpressed because his own magicians could also change water to blood.

Participant: Next there was an infestation of frogs, then swarms of lice, followed by wild beasts that invaded the Egyptian cities and homes. Then there was sickness among the Egyptian cattle, then the Egyptian people were afflicted with boils and sores and then there were hailstorms that ruined the crops. Each plague was more impressive then the last. Finally Pharaoh admitted that the Hebrew God was indeed a mighty and powerful force but still he would not let the Hebrews go.

Participant: Then came the plague of locusts that ate every green thing, and the plague of darkness that came at mid-day. After each of these plagues Pharaoh promised to let the Hebrews go. But each time he changed his mind. At last God said to Moses, "Tonight I will send one last plague upon Egypt. This time you must be ready to go immediately. "

Participant: It was the evening of the fourteenth day of the month of Nissan. Moses and Aaron had given us instructions. Each family marked their doorpost with the blood of the lamb they had eaten for their evening meal. Then at midnight a great mournful wail came from the palace. The prince, Pharaoh's first-born son, had died. Death had come to the first born son in every Egyptian house. But death had passed over every house where the doorpost had been marked with blood.

Participant: Soon messengers were knocking on every door. The Hebrews were told to set out at once. Pharaoh had agreed to let them go. The Hebrews did not even have time to let their bread rise. They had their first meal as free people in the dessert where they laid the dough on rocks and baked flat bread called Matzah. After several days journey they saw the Egyptian Army coming after them. Pharaoh had changed his mind again. They cried out to Moses, "Why have you brought us here to die in the wilderness?" Moses answered quietly, "Do not fear". As he spoke a cloud came down and hid the Hebrews from the Egyptians. Then Moses lifted his staff and stretched his hand out over the sea. The water spread apart, leaving a dry path. The Hebrews hurried along this path to the other side of the sea. The Egyptians followed them but when the Hebrews had all reached safety the waters came together again and the Egyptians were drowned.

Participant: Aaron and Miriam called to the Hebrew people to rejoice and sing songs of thanks. Miriam led the women in a dance. Then Moses called everyone together and said, "You must remember and never forget. When this time comes around each year, you and your children and your children's children will prepare a special feast to celebrate Passover. You will once again eat flat bread called Matzah. You will eat no leavened bread for seven days. When your children ask, 'Why is this night different from all other nights? You will say to them 'On this night God brought us out of Egypt from slavery to freedom.'"

Participant: From the Red Sea, our people traveled on to Mount Sinai where God gave them the Ten Commandments and the Torah. At Sinai, the Hebrews established a covenant with God, which sustains us to this day and teaches us to cherish a vision of the world free of Pharaohs, slavery and plagues.

Leader: Though we celebrate our liberation, our happiness cannot be complete so long as others had to be sacrificed for its sake. Therefore we pause and recall the plagues visited upon the Egyptians. We recite the list of these ten plagues, pouring off wine as each one is mentioned, diminishing the wine in our cups to give expression to our sorrow over the losses that each plague exacted.

Group: (Pour out a drop of wine to represent each plague)

Dam,	Blood	דָּם
Tzfardeyah,	Frogs	צְפַרְדֵּעַ
Kinim,	Lice	כִּנִּים
Arov,	Wild Beasts	עָרוֹב
Dever,	Blight	דֶּבֶר
Sh'chin,	Boils	שְׁחִין
Barad,	Hail	בָּרָד
Arbeh,	Locusts	אַרְבֶּה
Choshech,	Darkness	חֹשֶׁךְ
Makat B'chorot,	Death of the First-born.	מַכַּת בְּכוֹרוֹת

Leader: How many are the gifts Adonai our God has bestowed upon us!
Had Adonai brought us out of Egypt and not divided the sea for us, **Group:** Dayenu

Leader: Divided the sea and not permitted us to cross on dry land, **Group:** Dayenu
Leader: Permitted us to cross on dry land and not sustained us in the desert, **Group:** Dayenu
Leader: Sustained us for forty years in the desert and not fed us with manna, **Group:** Dayenu
Leader: Fed us with manna and not given us the Sabbath, **Group:** Dayenu
Leader: Given us the Sabbath and not brought us to Mount Sinai, **Group:** Dayenu
Leader: Brought us to Mount Sinai and not given us the Torah, **Group:** Dayenu
Leader: Given us the Torah and not led us into the land of Israel, **Group:** Dayenu
Leader: Led us into the land of Israel and not built for us the Temple, **Group:** Dayenu
Leader: Built for us the Temple and not sent us prophets of truth, **Group:** Dayenu
Leader: Sent us prophets of truth and not made us a holy people, **Group:** Dayenu
Leader: For all these--alone and together--we say:
Group: Dayenu!

Participant: What does this mean, "Dayenu, it would have been enough"? Surely no one of these would indeed have been enough for us. Dayenu means to celebrate each step toward freedom as if it were enough, then to start out on the next step. Dayenu means that if we reject each step because it is not the whole liberation, we will never be able to achieve the whole liberation. Dayenu means to sing each verse as if it were the whole song--and then sing the next verse!

All sing:
Da, da-yenu, da, da-yenu, da, da-yenu, dayenu, dayenu …

אִלּוּ הוֹצִיאָנוּ מִמִּצְרַיִם, דַּיֵּנוּ.

Ilu hotsi hotsianu,
hotsianu mi-Mitzrayim,
hotsianu mi-Mitzrayim, Dayenu.
Da, da-yenu, da, da-yenu, da, da-yenu,
dayenu, dayenu ...

אִלּוּ נָתַן לָנוּ אֶת־הַשַּׁבָּת, דַּיֵּנוּ.

Ilu natan natan lanu,
natan lanu et ha-Shabot,
natan lanu et ha-Shabot, Dayenu.
Da, da-yenu, da, da-yenu, da, da-yenu,
dayenu, dayenu ...

אִלּוּ נָתַן לָנוּ אֶת־הַתּוֹרָה, דַּיֵּנוּ.

Ilu natan natan lanu,
natan lanu et ha-Torah,
natan lanu et ha-Torah, Dayenu.
Da, da-yenu, da, da-yenu, da, da-yenu,
dayenu, dayenu ...

The Second Cup

Leader (optional): A Midrash relates that when the Egyptians were drowning in the Reed Sea, the angels wished to join in Israel's song of victory by singing "Halleluyah" but God rebuked them, saying: "How can you sing Halleluyah when My creatures are drowning?" In this spirit our wine has been diminished by our recitation of the ten plagues indicating our gladness is diminished by any human suffering, even the suffering of our enemies.

(The wine cups are raised.)

Group: Let us remember and never forget that our people have been delivered from oppressors again and again throughout the ages. For in every generation people have risen up to annihilate us. But each time we were delivered out of their hands.

Leader: Therefore, let us revere, exalt, extol, acclaim, adore and glorify the Holy One who performed these miracles for our ancestors and for us.

Group: Let us rejoice at the wonder of our deliverance:
from bondage to freedom,
from agony to joy,
from mourning to festivity,
from darkness to light,
from servitude to redemption.

We look forward to the celebration of a future redemption, the building of the City of Peace in which all people will rejoice and sing together a new song.

Leader: Therefore, let us say together,
Group: Halleluyah!

(Replace wine cups on the table)

Leader: In every generation, each person should feel as though he or she went forth from Egypt, as our Torah teaches: "And you shall explain to your child on that day, it is because of what God did for **me** when **I,** went forth from Egypt."
It was not just our ancestors who were redeemed but us as well, along with them, as it is written: "And God freed us from Egypt so as to take us and give us the land promised to our ancestors."

Participant (optional):

בְּכָל־דּוֹר וָדוֹר חַיָּב אָדָם לִרְאוֹת אֶת־עַצְמוֹ כְּאִלּוּ הוּא יָצָא מִמִּצְרָיִם.

B'chol dor v'dor chayav adam lirot et atzmo ki'eelu hu yatzah m'mitzrayim

Participant: The Exodus gave us our freedom. It also taught us our ethics, our theology, our philosophy of life. We know the heart of the stranger, the plight of the weak, the pain of the oppressed, the despair of the homeless, for we were strangers in the land of Egypt. And therefore, we recall these words as well:

Group: You shall not oppress a stranger, for you know the feelings of the stranger, having yourselves been strangers in Egypt.

Participant: When strangers reside with you in your land, you shall not wrong them… You shall love them as yourself, for you were strangers in Egypt. You shall rejoice before God with your son and daughter...and the stranger, and the orphan, and the widow in your midst. Remember and never forget that you were slaves in Egypt. You shall not subvert the rights of the stranger or the orphan. Remember that you were a slave in Egypt.

Participant (optional):
When Israel went forth from Egypt,
Jacob's household from a people of alien tongue.
Judah became His sanctuary, Israel His dominion.
The Sea saw and fled; the Jordan turned backward.
The mountains skipped like rams,
And the hills like young lambs.

What ails you, O Sea, that you flee?
O Jordan that you turn backward?
O mountain, that you skip like rams?
O hill like young lambs?

The presence of God makes the land tremble,
Makes the rock melt into water
And the cliffs spout fountains. (Psalm 114)

(All raise wine cups)

Group:
בָּרוּךְ אַתָּה יְיָ אֱלֹהֵינוּ מֶלֶךְ הָעוֹלָם בּוֹרֵא פְּרִי הַגָּפֶן.

Baruch Atah Adonai Eloheinu Melech ha-olam, borei p'ri ha-gafen.

We praise You, The Source of All That Exists,
Who creates the fruit of the vine!

(All drink the second cup of wine.)

Miriam's Cup

Leader: (Raise the empty goblet) Miriam's cup will be filled with water, rather than wine. I invite women of all generations at our Seder table to pour water from their own glasses into Miriam's cup.

(Pass Miriam's cup around the table).

A Midrash teaches us that a miraculous well accompanied the Hebrews throughout their journey in the desert, providing them with water. This well was given by G-d to Miriam, the prophetess, to honor her bravery and devotion to the Jewish people. Both Miriam and her well were sources of sustenance and healing. Her words of comfort gave the Hebrews the faith and confidence to overcome the hardships of the Exodus. We fill Miriam's cup with water to honor her role in ensuring the survival of the Jewish people. Like Miriam, Jewish women in all generations have been essential for the continuity of our people. As keepers of traditions in the home, women passed down songs and stories, rituals and recipes, from mother to daughter, from generation to generation. Let us each fill the cup of Miriam with water from our own glasses, so that our daughters may continue to draw from the strength and wisdom of our heritage.

(When Miriam's cup is filled, raise the goblet)

We place Miriam's cup on our Seder table to honor the important role of Jewish women in our tradition and history. Their stories also need to be told.

(Place the goblet in the middle of the table)

Pesach. Matzah. Maror

Leader: The Passover Seder is rich in symbolism, but there are three symbols that are so important and so meaningful that, in the words of Rabbi Gamaliel, grandson of Hillel, no Seder is really complete unless they are fully explained. These symbols are the pesach, the matzah, and the maror.

(Hold up the shank bone) What is the meaning of the pesach, the shank bone?

Participant: This bone is the symbol of the pesach lamb. After many years of wandering in the desert, the Israelites came to dwell in their own land, where each year, they would gather together at the Temple to celebrate the Exodus with rejoicing and festivity. Families would come from all parts of the land for the occasion, and each family would bring a lamb as its special offering in honor of the festival. This lamb was known as the pesach, in remembrance of the time when our ancestors were spared the tragic fate of the Egyptians, whose first-born were slain. For them, the pesach was a reminder that God "passed over" the houses of our ancestors in Egypt during the redemption.

Leader: (Point to the matzah) What is the meaning of the matzah?

Participant: Matzah reminds us of the dough our people baked the night they left Egypt. We left in such a hurry that we did not have time to allow the dough to rise.

Leader: (Point to the Maror) What is the meaning of the maror ?

Participant: We eat the maror, or bitter vegetables , to remind ourselves that the Egyptians embittered the lives of our people. Today, as well, wherever oppression remains, Jews taste its bitterness.

Leader: Pesach, matzah, and maror are the symbolic expressions that represent freedom in all ages. Translated into modern terms, they are sacrifice, preparedness, and remembrance. These are major elements in the battle for freedom.

RACHTZAH, Washing Our Hands

Leader: Before we eat we will wash our hands again and this time we will say the blessing together:

Group:

בָּרוּךְ אַתָּה יְיָ אֱלֹהֵינוּ מֶלֶךְ הָעוֹלָם אֲשֶׁר קִדְּשָׁנוּ בְּמִצְוֹתָיו וְצִוָּנוּ עַל נְטִילַת יָדָיִם.

Baruch Atah Adonai Eloheinu Melech ha-olam, asher kidshanu b'mitzvo-tav, v'tzivanu al n'tee-las yadayim.

We praise you, The Source of All that Exists,
Who hallows our lives with commandments and bids us wash our hands.

(The participants wash their hands. There is no speaking after hands are washed until the blessing for bread is said)

MOTZI, A Blessing for Bread

Leader: We are now coming to the Seder meal. As we ordinarily begin with the breaking of bread, we begin tonight with the breaking of matzah. We recite two blessings; first is the regular blessing for bread, then a special one for matzah.

(Pieces of the upper and lower pieces of the three matzot are distributed)

Group:

בָּרוּךְ אַתָּה יְיָ אֱלֹהֵינוּ מֶלֶךְ הָעוֹלָם הַמּוֹצִיא לֶחֶם מִן הָאָרֶץ.

Baruch Atah Adonai Eloheinu Melech ha-olam, ha-motzi lechem min ha-aretz.

We praise You, Source of All that Exists,
who brings forth bread from the earth.

MATZAH, A Special Blessing for Matzah

Group:

בָּרוּךְ אַתָּה יְיָ אֱלֹהֵינוּ מֶלֶךְ הָעוֹלָם אֲשֶׁר קִדְּשָׁנוּ בְּמִצְוֹתָיו
וְצִוָּנוּ עַל אֲכִילַת מַצָּה.

Baruch Atah Adonai Eloheinu Melech ha-olam, asher kidshanu b'mitzvo-ta,
v'tzivanu al a-chilat matzah.

We praise You, Source of All that Exists,
Who hallows our lives through commandments,
and commands us to eat matzah.

(Eat the portions of matzah)

MAROR, A Blessing for the Bitter Herbs

Leader: Now each of us will take a bit of the maror, the bitter herb, and dip it into the charoset to fulfill the commandment of this night to eat the maror. Thus, we dip our food the second time.

(Bitter herbs/vegetables are distributed and dipped into charoset)

Group:

בָּרוּךְ אַתָּה יְיָ אֱלֹהֵינוּ מֶלֶךְ הָעוֹלָם אֲשֶׁר קִדְּשָׁנוּ בְּמִצְוֹתָיו
וְצִוָּנוּ עַל אֲכִילַת מָרוֹר.

Baruch Atah Adonai Eloheinu Melech ha-olam asher kidshanu b'mitzvo-tav,
v'tzivanu al a-chilat maror.

We praise You, Source of All that Exists,
Who hallows our lives through commandments,
and commands us to eat maror.

(Eat the bitter herb/vegetable and charoset)

KORECH, The Hillel Sandwich

(Use matzah to make a sandwich with maror)

Leader: In the tradition of Hillel, we follow the custom of making a matzah and maror sandwich. We eat the maror of slavery together with the matzah of freedom. In times of slavery there is always the hope of freedom. In times of freedom, there is always the memory of slavery.

(Eat the maror sandwiched between two pieces of matzah.)

SHULCHAN ORECH, The Meal is Served

Leader: (Point to or hold up the roasted egg) It is customary to begin the meal with hard-boiled eggs flavored with salt water. The egg is symbolic of new life, and of hope. We even have a roasted egg on the Seder plate. This egg represents the festival offerings brought to the Ancient Temple in Jerusalem by the Hebrew people in thanksgiving for the fertility of their fields and flocks.

(Serve eggs)
(Remove the Haggadot and serve the meal)

(Toward the end of the meal, it is traditional to look for the afikoman, which has been hidden during the first part of the Seder. Whoever finds the afikoman may be offered a reward.)

TZAFUN,
The Afikoman is Found and Eaten

Leader: The second part of our Seder reflects our hopes and dreams. But we cannot begin until we have the afikomen that was hidden away during the first part of the Seder.

(Retrieve the afikomen from it's hiding place or offer a reward for its return. Then fit together the two pieces of matzah that were broken during the first half of the Seder)

Leader: What was broken is now made whole. What was hidden has been revealed. What was lost has now been found.

(Distribute the afikomen. Participants can eat their piece now or save it until after dessert. At some Seders nothing is eaten after the afikoman, so that the matzah is the last food tasted.)

(The third cup is filled.)

BARECH,
Thanks for Divine Sustenance

Leader: We have eaten our Passover meal as free people. Let us give thanks to the source of all life and freedom. Let us say grace.

Group (Hebrew is optional): בָּרוּךְ אַתָּה יְיָ הַזָּן אֶת־הַכֹּל.

Baruch ata Adonai ha-zan et ha-kol

Blessed is the Source of nourishment for all life.

Leader (Hebrew is optional): הָרַחֲמָן הוּא יִשְׁלַח לָנוּ בְּרָכָה
מְרֻבָּה בַּבַּיִת הַזֶּה וְעַל שֻׁלְחָן זֶה שֶׁאָכַלְנוּ עָלָיו.

Ha-rachaman Hu yishlach brachah m'roobah ba-bayit hazeh v'ahl shu;chan zeh she-achalnu alav.

May the Compassionate One send abundant blessings to this house and upon this table at which we have eaten.

Group (Hebrew is optional): הָרַחֲמָן הוּא יְבָרֵךְ הַבַּיִת הַזֶּה

Ha-rachaman. Hu y'varaych et ha-beyit ha-zey

May the Compassionate one bless this house.

Leader: עוֹשֶׂה שָׁלוֹם בִּמְרוֹמָיו הוּא יַעֲשֶׂה
שָׁלוֹם עָלֵינוּ וְעַל כָּל־יִשְׂרָאֵל וְאִמְרוּ אָמֵן.

Oseh shalom bim'rovam hu ya'aseh shalom aleinu v'al kol yisrael v'imru amen

May the One who brings harmony into the spheres on high bring peace to earth for all humanity.

Group (all sing): עוֹשֶׂה שָׁלוֹם בִּמְרוֹמָיו הוּא יַעֲשֶׂה
שָׁלוֹם עָלֵינוּ וְעַל כָּל־ יִשְׂרָאֵל וְאִמְרוּ אָמֵן.

Oseh shalom bim'romav hu ya'aseh shalom aleinu
v'al kol yisrael v'imru, v'imru amen
ya'aseh shalom ya'aseh shalom shalom aleinu v'al kol yisrael (x2)

The Third Cup

Leader: Together we take up the third cup of wine

(The wine cups are raised)

בָּרוּךְ אַתָּה יְיָ אֱלֹהֵינוּ מֶלֶךְ הָעוֹלָם בּוֹרֵא פְּרִי הַגָּפֶן.

Baruch Atah Adonai Eloheinu Melech ha-olam, borei p'ri ha-gafen.

We praise you, The Source of All That Exists,
Who creates the fruit of the vine!

(All drink the third cup of wine.)
(Fill the fourth cup)

Kos Eliyahu, the Cup of Elijah

Leader: This cup of wine is called "Kos Eliyahu" the cup of Elijah, a cup from which we cannot drink until the redemption is complete, until the world is whole and at peace, until justice and compassion reign where corruption and bigotry now hold sway. Elijah lived in the ninth century B.C.E. and devoted his life to challenging injustice and opposing idol worship. According to our legends, before he died, Elijah declared that he disguise himself and would return once each generation, coming to people's doors to see how he would be treated and to intervene in subtle and mysterious ways in the lives of the people he encountered.

Participant (optional): Elijah's cup symbolizes a time that has not yet come, but for which we yearn and pray. And lest we despair of that time ever arriving, let us take hope from the words of a child who had no reason to hope, yet did: "That's the difficulty in these times: ideals, dreams, and cherished hopes rise within us, only to meet the horrible truth and be shattered. It's really a wonder that I haven't dropped all my ideals, because they seem so absurd and impossible to carry out. Yet I keep them, because in spite of everything I still believe that people are really good at heart. I simply can't build up my hopes on a foundation consisting of confusion, misery and death. I see the world gradually being turned into a wilderness. I hear the ever-approaching thunder, which will destroy us too. I can feel the sufferings of millions and yet, if I look up into the heavens, I think that it will all come right, that this cruelty too will end, and that peace and tranquility will return again. In the meantime, I must uphold my ideals, for perhaps the time will come when I shall be able to carry them out." (From The Diary of Anne Frank)

Participant: In setting this cup at our table, we invite Elijah to join us, and we bring his passion for justice into our lives. According to Hasidic custom, we pass Elijah's cup from person to person at the table, each person pouring a little wine into Elijah's cup from our own cups, until it is filled. In this way we recognize that we must act together, each contributing our best talents and energies, to bring Elijah's promise to the world.

(Fill Elijah's cup, passing it around so all can contribute wine from their own cups.)

Participant (optional): An open door is an evocative image. We recall the times when we have been afraid to open our doors, the times when we were distrusted and were required to keep our doors open to surveillance and the times when we experienced terror because our doors were forced open by ignorant and hostile individuals. Tonight we will open our door wide and welcome Elijah into our home and into our hearts. May your message of a world redeemed from pain, injustice and hatred inspire us to become God's partners in the work of tikkun olam, repairing the world.

Group: Elijah opens up for us the realm of mystery and wonder. Let us now open the door for Elijah, and sing of the redemption Elijah will bring

(Someone is sent to open the door to the outside.)

All sing:

אֵלִיָּהוּ הַנָּבִיא, אֵלִיָּהוּ הַתִּשְׁבִּי,
אֵלִיָּהוּ, אֵלִיָּהוּ, אֵלִיָּהוּ הַגִּלְעָדִי,
בִּמְהֵרָה בְיָמֵינוּ יָבֹא אֵלֵינוּ עִם מָשִׁיחַ בֶּן דָּוִד.

Eliyahu ha-navi, Eliyahu ha-tishbi,
Eliyahu, Eliyahu, Eliyahu ha-giladi.

Bim-hei-rah be'yamenu, yavo eileinu,
im mashiach ben David, im mashiach ben David.

Eliyahu ha-navi, Eliyahu ha-tishbi,
Eliyahu, Eliyahu, Eliyahu ha-giladi.

Leader (optional): And may we live to see the day when nation shall not lift up sword against nation, nor will they prepare for war any more.

All sing (optional):

לֹא יִשָּׂא גוֹי אֶל גוֹי חֶרֶב
לֹא יִלְמְדוּ עוֹד מִלְחָמָה:

Lo yis'el goy el goy herev. Lo yimaldu al milchamah

Participant (optional): But that day is still far from sight. Ignorance, prejudice, hatred; contempt for truth and justice; hunger and terror; the fear of a world-destroying disaster--these remain to plague the human race. To end these plagues, to summon Elijah--that is our task, for we are the people who know the stranger's heart, the slave's aching bones, the shaking hands of the exile. When will Elijah come with the news of freedom?

Group (optional): When we have called him by our deeds.

HALLEL

Leader (optional: At this point in the Seder it is traditional to sing songs of praise. Praise is an expression of faith. We give voice to our faith in a Single Source of All that Exists. We invite all who live on earth to join us in a song that expresses our belief that a spark of that Single Source is within each and every human being making it possible for human beings to triumph over the powers of destruction.

Participant or Group (optional):

Hallelu et Adonai kol goyim *shachuhu kiol ha'umim.*
Ki gavar aleinu chasdo *v'emet Adonai l'olam halleluyah*

Hodu l'Adonai ki tov *ki l'olam chasdo.*
Yomar-na Yisrael *ki l'olam chasdo.*
Yomru-na vet Aoron *ki l'olam chasdo.*
Yomru-na yir'ei Adonai *ki l'olam chasdo.*

הַלְלוּ אֶת־יְיָ כָּל־גּוֹיִם, שַׁבְּחוּהוּ כָּל־הָאֻמִּים.
כִּי גָבַר עָלֵינוּ חַסְדּוֹ, וֶאֱמֶת יְיָ לְעוֹלָם. הַלְלוּיָהּ.

הוֹדוּ לַייָ כִּי־טוֹב כִּי לְעוֹלָם חַסְדּוֹ.
יֹאמַר־נָא יִשְׂרָאֵל כִּי לְעוֹלָם חַסְדּוֹ.
יֹאמְרוּ נָא בֵית אַהֲרֹן כִּי לְעוֹלָם חַסְדּוֹ.
יֹאמְרוּ נָא יִרְאֵי יְיָ כִּי לְעוֹלָם חַסְדּוֹ.

Praise the Lord, all ye nations; Praise him, all ye people of the earth.
For great is his mercy upon us; And the truth of the Lord is everlasting

Give thanks to the Lord for he is good: For his lovingkindness endures forever.
Let Israel say: For his lovingkindness endures forever.
Let the house of Aaron say: For his lovingkindness endures forever.
Let them that revere the Lord say: For his lovingkindness endures forever.

The Fourth Cup

Leader: As our Seder draws to an end, we take up our cups one last time. The redemption is not yet complete. Not everyone in our world is yet free. This fourth cup reminds us of our responsibility to be God's partners in bringing freedom to those enslaved, peace to those at war, food to those who hunger. This is our purpose as Jews. May we live to fulfill it.

(The wine cups are raised)

Group:

בָּרוּךְ אַתָּה יְיָ אֱלֹהֵינוּ מֶלֶךְ הָעוֹלָם בּוֹרֵא פְּרִי הַגָּפֶן.

Baruch Atah Adonai Eloheinu Melech ha-olam, borei p'ri ha-gafen.

We praise you, The Source of All That Exists,
Who creates the fruit of the vine!

(All drink the fourth cup of wine.)

NIRTZAH, Conclusion

Leader: The Seder is now concluded, its rites observed in full, its purposes revealed. As we gathered together to celebrate this seder tonight, may we be worthy to celebrate again in freedom next year. And may God, who redeemed our ancestors from slavery and degradation, redeem all who are enslaved and bring freedom and dignity to our entire world. Together, let us say:

לַשָּׁנָה הַבָּאָה בִּירוּשָׁלָיִם.

Group:

L'sha-nah ha-ba-ah bi-ru-sha-la-yim!

Next year in Jerusalem

שִׁירִים

Chad Gadya

Chad gadya, chad gadya.
Dizabin aba bit'rei zuzei. Chad gadya, chad gadya.

Ve'ata shunra, ve'achla le'gadya,
Dizabin aba bit'rei zuzei. Chad gadya, chad gadya.

Ve'ata chalba, ve'nashach leshunra, de'achla le'gadya,
Dizabin aba bit'rei zuzei. Chad gadya, chad gadya.

Ve'ata chutra, ve'hika le'chalba, de'nashach le'shunra, ve'achla le'gadya,
Dizabin aba bit'rei zuzei. Chad gadya, chad gadya.

Ve'ata nura, ve'saraf le'chutra, de'hika le'chalba, de'nashach leshunra,
de''achla le'gadya,
Dizabin aba bit'rei zuzei. Chad gadya, chad gadya.

Ve'ata maya, ve'chaba le'nura, de'saraf le'chutra, de'hika le'chalba,
de'nashach le'shunra, de'achla le'gadya,
Dizabin aba bit'rei zuzei. Chad gadya, chad gadya.

Ve'ata tora, ve'shata le'maya, ve'chaba le'nura, de'saraf le'chutra,
de'hika le'chalba, de'nashach le'shunra, de'achla le'gadya,
Dizabin aba bit'rei zuzei. Chad gadya, chad gadya.

Ve'ata ha'shochet, ve'shachat le'tora, de'shata le'maya, ve'chaba le'nura, de'saraf
le'chutra, de'hika le'chalba, de'nashach le'shunra, de'achla le'gadya,
Dizabin aba bit'rei zuzei. Chad gadya, chad gadya.

Ve'ata malach hamavet, ve'shachat le'shochet, de'shachat le'tora, de'shata le'maya,
ve'chaba le'nura, de'saraf le'chutra, de'hika le'chalba, de'nashach le'shunra, de'achla
le'gadya,
Dizabin aba bit'rei zuzei. Chad gadya, chad gady a.

Ve'ata HaKadosh Baruch Hu, vishachat le'malach hamavet, de'shachat le'shochet,
de'shachat le'tora, de'shata le'maya, ve'chaba le'nura, de'saraf le'chutra, de'hika
le'chalba, de'nashach le'shunra, de'achla le'gadya,
Dizabin aba bit'rei zuzei. Chad gadya, chad gadya.

חַד גַּדְיָא

חַד גַּדְיָא, חַד גַּדְיָא,
דִּזְבַן אַבָּא בִּתְרֵי זוּזֵי;
חַד גַּדְיָא, חַד גַּדְיָא,

וְאָתָא שׁוּנְרָא וְאָכַל לְגַדְיָא,
דִּזְבַן אַבָּא בִּתְרֵי זוּזֵי;
חַד גַּדְיָא, חַד גַּדְיָא.

וְאָתָא כַלְבָּא וְנָשַׁךְ לְשׁוּנְרָא,
דְּאָכַל לְגַדְיָא, דִּזְבַן אַבָּא בִּתְרֵי זוּזֵי;
חַד גַּדְיָא, חַד גַּדְיָא.

וְאָתָא חוּטְרָא וְהִכָּה לְכַלְבָּא,
דְּנָשַׁךְ לְשׁוּנְרָא, דְּאָכַל לְגַדְיָא,
דִּזְבַן אַבָּא בִּתְרֵי זוּזֵי;
חַד גַּדְיָא, חַד גַּדְיָא.

וְאָתָא נוּרָא וְשָׂרַף לְחוּטְרָא,
דְּהִכָּה לְכַלְבָּא, דְּנָשַׁךְ לְשׁוּנְרָא,
דְּאָכַל לְגַדְיָא, דִּזְבַן אַבָּא בִּתְרֵי זוּזֵי;
חַד גַּדְיָא, חַד גַּדְיָא.

וְאָתָא מַיָּא וְכָבָה לְנוּרָא,
דְּשָׂרַף לְחוּטְרָא, דְּהִכָּה לְכַלְבָּא,
דְּנָשַׁךְ לְשׁוּנְרָא, דְּאָכַל לְגַדְיָא,
דִּזְבַן אַבָּא בִּתְרֵי זוּזֵי;
חַד גַּדְיָא, חַד גַּדְיָא.

וְאָתָא תוֹרָא וְשָׁתָא לְמַיָּא,
דְּכָבָה לְנוּרָא, דְּשָׂרַף לְחוּטְרָא,
דְּהִכָּה לְכַלְבָּא, דְּנָשַׁךְ לְשׁוּנְרָא,
דְּאָכַל לְגַדְיָא, דִּזְבַן אַבָּא בִּתְרֵי זוּזֵי;
חַד גַּדְיָא, חַד גַּדְיָא.

וְאָתָא הַשּׁוֹחֵט וְשָׁחַט לְתוֹרָא,
דְּשָׁתָה לְמַיָּא, דְּכָבָה לְנוּרָא,
דְּשָׂרַף לְחוּטְרָא, דְּהִכָּה לְכַלְבָּא,
דְּנָשַׁךְ לְשׁוּנְרָא, דְּאָכַל לְגַדְיָא,
דִּזְבַן אַבָּא בִּתְרֵי זוּזֵי;
חַד גַּדְיָא, חַד גַּדְיָא.

וְאָתָא מַלְאַךְ הַמָּוֶת, וְשָׁחַט לַשּׁוֹחֵט,
דְּשָׁחַט לְתוֹרָא, דְּשָׁתָה לְמַיָּא,
דְּכָבָה לְנוּרָא, דְּשָׂרַף לְחוּטְרָא,
דְּהִכָּה לְכַלְבָּא, דְּנָשַׁךְ לְשׁוּנְרָא,
דְּאָכַל לְגַדְיָא, דִּזְבַן אַבָּא בִּתְרֵי זוּזֵי;
חַד גַּדְיָא, חַד גַּדְיָא.

וְאָתָא הַקָּדוֹשׁ בָּרוּךְ הוּא, וְשָׁחַט לְמַלְאַךְ הַמָּוֶת,
דְּשָׁחַט לַשּׁוֹחֵט, דְּשָׁחַט לְתוֹרָא,
דְּשָׁתָה לְמַיָּא, דְּכָבָה לְנוּרָא,
דְּשָׂרַף לְחוּטְרָא, דְּהִכָּה לְכַלְבָּא,
דְּנָשַׁךְ לְשׁוּנְרָא, דְּאָכַל לְגַדְיָא,
דִּזְבַן אַבָּא בִּתְרֵי זוּזֵי;
חַד גַּדְיָא, חַד גַּדְיָא.

One kid, one kid my father bought for two zuzim,

. . .And then came the Holy One, blessed be God and destroyed the angel of death that slew the butcher,that killed the ox, that drank the water, that quenched the fire, that burned the stick,that beat the dog, that bit the cat, that ate the kid my father bought for two zuzim , One kid, one kid

Adir Hu

Adir hu, adir hu, yivneh veito b'karov.
Bimheira, bimheira, b'yameinu b'karov.
Eil b'nei, eil b'nei, Eil b'nei b'karov
Bimheira, bimheira, b'yameinu b'karov.

Mighty is He, noble is He,
He will soon build up His dwelling
And in haste, with all speed
In our time come to build, build thy dwelling, very soon!

אַדִּיר הוּא. אַדִּיר הוּא.
יִבְנֶה בֵיתוֹ בְּקָרוֹב.
בִּמְהֵרָה. בִּמְהֵרָה.
בְּיָמֵינוּ בְּקָרוֹב.
אֵל בְּנֵה. אֵל בְּנֵה.
בְּנֵה בֵיתְךָ בְּקָר

Hiney Ma-Tov

Hiney ma-tov umah-nayim shevet achim gam-yachad

הִנֵּה מַה־טּוֹב וּמַה־נָּעִים שֶׁבֶת אַחִים גַּם־יָחַד׃

How good and how pleasant for brethren to dwell in harmony

Esa Eynai (psalm 121:1-2)

Esa eynai el heharim me'ayin yavo ezri (x2)
Ezri me'im adonai
oseh shamayim va'oretz (x2)

I lift my eyes to the hills
My help comes from there
My help comes from God
Who makes heaven and earth

אֶשָּׂא עֵינַי אֶל־הֶהָרִים
מֵאַיִן יָבוֹא עֶזְרִי׃
עֶזְרִי מֵעִם יהוה
עֹשֵׂה שָׁמַיִם וָאָרֶץ׃

Mah Gadlu (psalm 92)

Mah-gadlu ma-asey-cha Ya. M'od amku mach-sh'vo-techa

מַה־גָּדְלוּ מַעֲשֶׂיךָ יְהוָה מְאֹד עָמְקוּ מַחְשְׁבֹתֶיךָ׃

How great are thy deeds, Thy thoughts are very profound.

Eleh Chamdah Libi

Eleh chamdah libi, chusa na v'al tit-alom
Eleh chamdah, chamdah libi chusa na v'al tit-alom

אֱלֶה חָמְדָה לִבִּי. חוּסָה נָּא וְאַל תִּתְעַלָּם:

A yearning heart cries out to God, "Lord, love us; do not forsake us."

Oseh Shalom

Oseh shalom bim'rovam hu ya'aseh shalom aleinu
v'al kol yisrael v'imru amen

עוֹשֶׂה שָׁלוֹם בִּמְרוֹמָיו הוּא יַעֲשֶׂה שָׁלוֹם עָלֵינוּ וְעַל כָּל-
יִשְׂרָאֵל וְאִמְרוּ אָמֵן.

May the One who brings harmony
to the spheres on high bring peace to earth for all humanity.

Yisma-chu Hashamayim

Yisma-chu Hashamayim (3x)
Vetagel ha'aretz
Yiram hayam (3x) umelo'o.
Yiram hayam (3x) umelo'o.

יִשְׂמְחוּ הַשָּׁמַיִם
וְתָגֵל הָאָרֶץ
יִרְעַם הַיָּם וּמְלֹאוֹ:

Let the heaven rejoice and the earth be glad,
The sea exult in its fullness.
(psalm 96.11)

Lo Yisa Goy

Lo yisa goy el goy cherev
Lo yilmedu od milchamah

לֹא יִשָּׂא גוֹי אֶל גוֹי חֶרֶב
לֹא יִלְמְדוּ עוֹד מִלְחָמָה:

Nation shall not lift up sword against nation.
Neither will they learn war anymore. (Isaiah 2:4)

Heveynu Shalom Aleychem

Heveynu shalom aleychem (x3)
Heveynu shalom shalom shalom aleychem!

הֵבֵאנוּ שָׁלוֹם עֲלֵיכֶם.

We brought peace unto you!

Hava Nagila

Hava Nagila (x3) V'nis m'cha!
Hava n'ra n'na (x3) V'nis m'cha!

Uru
Uru achim b'lev sameach (x3)
Uru achim. . . .
B'lev sameach!

הָבָה נָגִילָה, וְנִשְׂמְחָה.
הָבָה נְרַנְּנָה, וְנִשְׂמְחָה.
עוּרוּ אַחִים בְּלֵב שָׂמֵחַ.

Bring on the music! And let's have fun!
Start up the dancing too! And let's have fun
Sing out, sing out brothers.
With joy in your hearts!

Mayim, Mayim

Ushevatem mayim b'sason mi-mayenei hayeshuah (x2)
mayim mayim mayim mayim hey mayim b'sason (x2)
Hey hey hey hey
mayim mayim mayim mayim hei mayim b'sason (x2)

וּשְׁאַבְתֶּם מַיִם בְּשָׂשׂוֹן מִמַּעַיְנֵי הַיְשׁוּעָה
מַיִם, מַיִם, מַיִם, מַיִם הֵי מַיִם בְּשָׂשׂוֹן
הֵי, הֵי, הֵי, הֵי
מַיִם, מַיִם, מַיִם, מַיִם מַיִם, מַיִם, בְּשָׂשׂוֹן

Draw up water with joy from the well of salvation

Echad Mi Yodeah -- Who Knows One?

Echad, mi yode'a? Echad ani yode'a.
Echad Eloheinu she'bashamayim uva'aretz.

Shnayim, mi yode'a? Shanayim ani yode'a.
Sh'nei luchot habrit, echad Eloheinu she'bashamayim uva'aretz.

Shlosha, mi yode'a? Shlosha ani yode'a.
Sh'losha avot, sh'nei luchot habrit, echad Eloheinu she'bashamayim uva'aretz.

Arba, mi yode'a? Arba ani yode'a.
Arba imahot, sh'losha avot, sh'nei luchot habrit, echad Eloheinu she'bashamayim uva'aretz.

Chamisha mi yode'a? Chamisha ani yode'a.
Hamisha chumshei Torah, arba imahot, sh'losha avot, sh'nei luchot habrit, echad Eloheinu she'bashamayim uva'aretz.

Shisha mi yode'a? Shisha ani yode'a.
Shisha sidrei mishna, Hamisha chumshei Torah, arba imahot, sh'losha avot, sh'nei luchot habrit, echad Eloheinu she'bashamayim uva'aretz.

Shiva mi yode'a? Shiva ani yode'a.
Shiva y'mei shabb'ta, shisha sidrei mishna, hamisha chumshei Torah, arba imahot, sh'losha avot, sh'nei luchot habrit, echad Eloheinu she'bashamayim uva'aretz.

Shmona mi yode'a? Shmona ani yode'a.
Sh'mona y'mei milah, shiva y'mei shabb'ta, shisha sidrei mishna, hamisha chumshei Torah, arba imahot, sh'losha avot, sh'nei luchot habrit, echad Eloheinu she'bashamayim uva'aretz.

Tisha mi yode'a? Tisha ani yode'a.
Tisha yarhei leidah, sh'mona y'mei milah, shiva y'mei shabb'ta, shisha sidrei mishna, hamisha chumshei Torah, arba imahot, sh'losha avot, sh'nei luchot habrit, echad Eloheinu she'bashamayim uva'aretz.

Asara mi yode'a? Asara ani yode'a.
Asara dibraya, tisha yarhei leidah, sh'mona y'mei milah, shiva y'mei shabb'ta, shisha sidrei mishna, hamisha chumshei Torah, arba imahot, sh'losha avot, sh'nei luchot habrit, echad Eloheinu she'bashamayim uva'aretz.

Achad mi yode'a? Achad ani yode'a.
Achad-asar kokhvaya, asara dibraya, tisha yarhei leidah, sh'mona y'mei milah, shiva y'mei shabb'ta, shisha sidrei mishna, hamisha chumshei Torah, arba imahot, sh'losha avot, sh'nei luchot habrit, echad Eloheinu she'bashamayim uva'aretz.

Shneim mi yode'a? Shneim ani yode'a.

Shneim-asar shivtaya, achad-asar kokhvaya, asara dibraya, tisha yarhei leidah, sh'mona y'mei milah, shiva y'mei shabb'ta, shisha sidrei mishna, hamisha chumshei Torah, arba imahot, sh'losha avot, sh'nei luchot habrit, echad Eloheinu she'bashamayim uva'aretz.

Sh'losha mi yode'a? Sh'losha ani yode'a.
Sh'losha-asar midaya, shneim-asar shivtaya, achad-asar kokhvaya, asara dibraya, tisha yarhei leidah, sh'mona y'mei milah, shiva y'mei shabb'ta, shisha sidrei mishna, hamisha chumshei Torah, arba imahot, sh'losha avot, sh'nei luchot habrit, echad Eloheinu she'bashamayim uva'aretz.

(Hebrew text and English translation can be found on the following pages)

אֶחָד מִי יוֹדֵעַ

Who knows one?
I know one:
One is God of heaven and earth.

אֶחָד מִי יוֹדֵעַ? אֶחָד אֲנִי יוֹדֵעַ: אֶחָד
אֱלֹהֵינוּ שֶׁבַּשָּׁמַיִם וּבָאָרֶץ.

Who knows two?
I know two.
Two stone tablets of the Law;
One is God of heaven and earth.

שְׁנַיִם מִי יוֹדֵעַ? שְׁנַיִם אֲנִי יוֹדֵעַ: שְׁנֵי
לֻחוֹת הַבְּרִית, אֶחָד אֱלֹהֵינוּ
שֶׁבַּשָּׁמַיִם וּבָאָרֶץ.

Who knows three?
I know three:
Three believing Patriarchs;
Two stone tablets of the Law;
One is God of heaven and earth.

שְׁלוֹשָׁה מִי יוֹדֵעַ? שְׁלוֹשָׁה אֲנִי יוֹדֵעַ:
שְׁלוֹשָׁה אָבוֹת, שְׁנֵי לֻחוֹת הַבְּרִית,
אֶחָד אֱלֹהֵינוּ שֶׁבַּשָּׁמַיִם וּבָאָרֶץ.

Who knows four?
I know four:
Four fruitful Matriarchs;
Three believing Patriarchs;
Two stone tablets of the Law;
One is God of heaven and earth.

אַרְבַּע מִי יוֹדֵעַ? אַרְבַּע אֲנִי יוֹדֵעַ:
אַרְבַּע אִמָּהוֹת, שְׁלוֹשָׁה אָבוֹת, שְׁנֵי
לֻחוֹת הַבְּרִית, אֶחָד אֱלֹהֵינוּ
שֶׁבַּשָּׁמַיִם וּבָאָרֶץ.

Who knows five?
I know five:
Five the Books of Moses;
Four fruitful Matriarchs;
Three believing Patriarchs;
Two stone tablets of the Law;
One is God of heaven and earth.

חֲמִשָּׁה מִי יוֹדֵעַ? חֲמִשָּׁה אֲנִי יוֹדֵעַ:
חֲמִשָּׁה חֻמְשֵׁי תוֹרָה, אַרְבַּע אִמָּהוֹת,
שְׁלוֹשָׁה אָבוֹת, שְׁנֵי לֻחוֹת הַבְּרִית,
אֶחָד אֱלֹהֵינוּ שֶׁבַּשָּׁמַיִם וּבָאָרֶץ.

Who knows six?
I know six:
Six sections of Mishnah;
Five the Books of Moses;
Four fruitful Matriarchs;
Three believing Patriarchs;
Two stone tablets of the Law;
One is God of heaven and earth.

שִׁשָּׁה מִי יוֹדֵעַ? שִׁשָּׁה אֲנִי יוֹדֵעַ:
שִׁשָּׁה סִדְרֵי מִשְׁנָה, חֲמִשָּׁה חֻמְשֵׁי
תוֹרָה, אַרְבַּע אִמָּהוֹת, שְׁלוֹשָׁה
אָבוֹת, שְׁנֵי לֻחוֹת הַבְּרִית, אֶחָד
אֱלֹהֵינוּ שֶׁבַּשָּׁמַיִם וּבָאָרֶץ.

Who knows seven?
I know seven:
Seven days of the week;
Six sections of Mishnah;
Five the Books of Moses;
Four fruitful Matriarchs;
Three believing Patriarchs;
Two stone tablets of the Law;
One is God of heaven and earth.

שִׁבְעָה מִי יוֹדֵעַ? שִׁבְעָה אֲנִי יוֹדֵעַ:
שִׁבְעָה יְמֵי שַׁבַּתָּא, שִׁשָּׁה סִדְרֵי
מִשְׁנָה, חֲמִשָּׁה חֻמְשֵׁי תוֹרָה, אַרְבַּע
אִמָּהוֹת, שְׁלוֹשָׁה אָבוֹת, שְׁנֵי לֻחוֹת
הַבְּרִית, אֶחָד אֱלֹהֵינוּ שֶׁבַּשָּׁמַיִם
וּבָאָרֶץ.

Who knows eight?
I know eight:
Eight days before the foreskin's cut;
Seven days of the week;
Six sections of Mishnah;
Five the Books of Moses;
Four fruitful Matriarchs;
Three believing Patriarchs;
Two stone tablets of the Law;
One is God of heaven and earth.

שְׁמוֹנָה מִי יוֹדֵעַ? שְׁמוֹנָה אֲנִי יוֹדֵעַ:
שְׁמוֹנָה יְמֵי מִילָה, שִׁבְעָה יְמֵי
שַׁבַּתָּא, שִׁשָּׁה סִדְרֵי מִשְׁנָה, חֲמִשָּׁה
חֻמְשֵׁי תוֹרָה, אַרְבַּע אִמָּהוֹת,
שְׁלוֹשָׁה אָבוֹת, שְׁנֵי לֻחוֹת הַבְּרִית,
אֶחָד אֱלֹהֵינוּ שֶׁבַּשָּׁמַיִם וּבָאָרֶץ.

Who knows nine?
I know nine:
Nine months to make a human child;
Eight days before the foreskin's cut;
Seven days of the week;
Six sections of Mishnah;
Five the Books of Moses;
Four fruitful Matriarchs;
Three believing Patriarchs;
Two stone tablets of the Law;
One is God of heaven and earth.

תִּשְׁעָה מִי יוֹדֵעַ? תִּשְׁעָה אֲנִי יוֹדֵעַ:
תִּשְׁעָה יַרְחֵי לֵדָה, שְׁמוֹנָה יְמֵי
מִילָה, שִׁבְעָה יְמֵי שַׁבַּתָּא, שִׁשָּׁה
סִדְרֵי מִשְׁנָה, חֲמִשָּׁה חֻמְשֵׁי תוֹרָה,
אַרְבַּע אִמָּהוֹת, שְׁלוֹשָׁה אָבוֹת, שְׁנֵי
לֻחוֹת הַבְּרִית, אֶחָד אֱלֹהֵינוּ
שֶׁבַּשָּׁמַיִם וּבָאָרֶץ.

Who knows ten?
I know ten:
Ten, the Ten Commandments;
Nine months to make a human child;
Eight days before the foreskin's cut;
Seven days of the week;
Six sections of Mishnah;
Five the Books of Moses;
Four fruitful Matriarchs;
Three believing Patriarchs;
Two stone tablets of the Law;
One is God of heaven and earth.

עֲשָׂרָה מִי יוֹדֵעַ? עֲשָׂרָה אֲנִי יוֹדֵעַ:
עֲשָׂרָה דִבְּרַיָּא, תִּשְׁעָה יַרְחֵי לֵדָה,
שְׁמוֹנָה יְמֵי מִילָה, שִׁבְעָה יְמֵי
שַׁבַּתָּא, שִׁשָּׁה סִדְרֵי מִשְׁנָה, חֲמִשָּׁה
חֻמְשֵׁי תוֹרָה, אַרְבַּע אִמָּהוֹת,
שְׁלוֹשָׁה אָבוֹת, שְׁנֵי לֻחוֹת הַבְּרִית,
אֶחָד אֱלֹהֵינוּ שֶׁבַּשָּׁמַיִם וּבָאָרֶץ.

Who knows eleven?
I know eleven:
Eleven stars in Joseph's dream;
Ten, the Ten Commandments;
Nine months to make a human child;
Eight days before the foreskin's cut;
Seven days of the week;
Six sections of Mishnah;
Five the Books of Moses;
Four fruitful Matriarchs;
Three believing Patriarchs;
Two stone tablets of the Law;
One is God of heaven and earth.

אַחַד עָשָׂר מִי יוֹדֵעַ? אַחַד עָשָׂר אֲנִי
יוֹדֵעַ: אַחַד עָשָׂר כּוֹכְבַיָּא, עֲשָׂרָה
דִבְּרַיָּא, תִּשְׁעָה יַרְחֵי לֵדָה, שְׁמוֹנָה
יְמֵי מִילָה, שִׁבְעָה יְמֵי שַׁבַּתָּא, שִׁשָּׁה
סִדְרֵי מִשְׁנָה, חֲמִשָּׁה חֻמְשֵׁי תוֹרָה,
אַרְבַּע אִמָּהוֹת, שְׁלוֹשָׁה אָבוֹת, שְׁנֵי
לֻחוֹת הַבְּרִית, אֶחָד אֱלֹהֵינוּ
שֶׁבַּשָּׁמַיִם וּבָאָרֶץ.

Who knows twelve?
I know twelve:
Twelve tribes of Israel;
Eleven stars in Joseph's dream;
Ten, the Ten Commandments;
Nine months to make a human child;
Eight days before the foreskin's cut;
Seven days of the week;
Six sections of Mishnah;
Five the Books of Moses;
Four fruitful Matriarchs;
Three believing Patriarchs;
Two stone tablets of the Law;
One is God of heaven and earth.

שְׁנֵים עָשָׂר מִי יוֹדֵעַ? שְׁנֵים עָשָׂר אֲנִי
יוֹדֵעַ: שְׁנֵים עָשָׂר שִׁבְטַיָּא, אַחַד
עָשָׂר כּוֹכְבַיָּא, עֲשָׂרָה דִבְּרַיָּא, תִּשְׁעָה
יַרְחֵי לֵדָה, שְׁמוֹנָה יְמֵי מִילָה, שִׁבְעָה
יְמֵי שַׁבַּתָּא, שִׁשָּׁה סִדְרֵי מִשְׁנָה,
חֲמִשָּׁה חֻמְשֵׁי תוֹרָה, אַרְבַּע אִמָּהוֹת,
שְׁלוֹשָׁה אָבוֹת, שְׁנֵי לֻחוֹת הַבְּרִית,
אֶחָד אֱלֹהֵינוּ שֶׁבַּשָּׁמַיִם וּבָאָרֶץ.

Who knows thirteen?
I know thirteen:
Thirteen attributes of God;
Twelve tribes of Israel;
Eleven stars in Joseph's dream;
Ten, the Ten Commandments;
Nine months to make a human child;
Eight days before the foreskin's cut;
Seven days of the week;
Six sections of Mishnah;
Five the Books of Moses;
Four fruitful Matriarchs;
Three believing Patriarchs;
Two stone tablets of the Law;
One is God of heaven and earth.

שְׁלוֹשָׁה עָשָׂר מִי יוֹדֵעַ? שְׁלוֹשָׁה עָשָׂר
אֲנִי יוֹדֵעַ: שְׁלוֹשָׁה עָשָׂר מִדַּיָּא, שְׁנֵים
עָשָׂר שִׁבְטַיָּא, אַחַד עָשָׂר כּוֹכְבַיָּא,
עֲשָׂרָה דִבְּרַיָּא, תִּשְׁעָה יַרְחֵי לֵדָה,
שְׁמוֹנָה יְמֵי מִילָה, שִׁבְעָה יְמֵי
שַׁבַּתָּא, שִׁשָּׁה סִדְרֵי מִשְׁנָה, חֲמִשָּׁה
חֻמְשֵׁי תוֹרָה, אַרְבַּע אִמָּהוֹת,
שְׁלוֹשָׁה אָבוֹת, שְׁנֵי לֻחוֹת הַבְּרִית,
אֶחָד אֱלֹהֵינוּ שֶׁבַּשָּׁמַיִם וּבָאָרֶץ.

www.ingramcontent.com/pod-product-compliance
Ingram Content Group UK Ltd.
Pitfield, Milton Keynes, MK11 3LW, UK
UKHW051134260726
13967UKWH00010B/3052